CREATIVE LIVES

Barbara Hepworth

ANDREW LANGLEY

www.heinemann.co.uk/library
Visit our website to find out more information about **Heinemann Library** books.

To order:
☎ Phone 44 (0) 1865 888066
▤ Send a fax to 44 (0) 1865 314091
🖳 Visit the Heinemann Bookshop at www.heinemann.co.uk/library to browse our catalogue and order online.

First published in Great Britain by Heinemann Library, Halley Court, Jordan Hill, Oxford OX2 8EJ, a division of Reed Educational and Professional Publishing Ltd. Heinemann is a registered trademark of Reed Educational and Professional Publishing Ltd.

OXFORD MELBOURNE AUCKLAND JOHANNESBURG BLANTYRE
GABORONE IBADAN PORTSMOUTH NH (USA) CHICAGO

© Reed Educational and Professional Publishing Ltd 2002
The moral right of the proprietor has been asserted.

Designed by Tinstar Design (www.tinstar.co.uk)
Originated by Ambassador Litho Ltd
Printed and bound by South China Printing Comapny Ltd in Hong Kong/China

ISBN 0 431 13997 0
06 05 04 03 02
10 9 8 7 6 5 4 3 2 1

British Library Cataloguing in Publication Data
Langley, Andrew
       Barbara Hepworth. – (Creative Lives)
       1. Hepworth, Barbara, 1903–1975
       2. Women sculptors – England – Biography – Juvenile literature
       3. Sculptors – England – Biography – Juvenile literature
       I.Title
       730.9'2

Acknowledgements
The Publishers would like to thank the following for permission to reproduce photographs: Alan Bowness, Hepworth Estate: pp5, 8, 9, 10, 13, 17, 21, 35, 38, 41, 44, 49; BBC Photograph Library: p43; Bridgeman Art Library/Manchester City Art Galleries: p15; Hulton Getty Picture Collection: pp14, 19, 37, 51; Popperfoto: pp32, 40, 42, 52; Royal Collection Picture Library: p46; Tate Collection: p7; Tate Gallery Archive: pp6, 11, 16, 20, 22, 23, 24, 25, 26, 28, 50; Tate Gallery St Ives: pp33, 39, 55; Tate Picture Library: pp18, 31; Topham Picturepoint: pp4, 45, 48.

Cover photograph reproduced with permission of Topham Picturepoint.

Picture research by Kay Altwegg.

Our thanks to Sir Alan Bowness and Matthew Gale for their assistance in the preparation of this book.

Every effort has been made to contact copyright holders of any material reproduced in this book. Any omissions will be rectified in subsequent printings if notice is given to the Publishers.

Contents

Any words appearing in the text in bold, **like this**, are explained in the Glossary.

The first great woman sculptor

On 10 January 1973, there was a very special birthday party. It took place in St Ives, Cornwall, and was to celebrate the 70th year of Dame Barbara Hepworth, one of the most famous British artists of the 20th century. At dinner, a close friend and neighbour rose to propose a toast – to the 'first great woman sculptor'.

On the face of it, this was a very big claim. There had been sculptors at work all over the world for more than 5000 years. Although the vast majority of them had been men, surely there must have been a great female sculptor before Hepworth? But the friend was right. Women sculptors are almost invisible in the long history of art. Only the tragic figure of Camille Claudel stands out – a Frenchwoman who fought hard to establish herself in the art world of 1890s Paris before falling prey to madness. Sculpture, more than any other branch of the arts, is usually seen as a man's world. You need muscles to handle and carve hefty blocks of stone or wood, or to prepare **bronzes** for **casting**.

Barbara Hepworth with one of her large 'abstract' sculptures. The form is not copied from nature, but explores pure shapes and spaces – both inside and out.

> " *Sculpture is to me an affirmative statement of our will to live: whether it be small, to rest in the hand; or larger, to be embraced; or larger still, to force us to move around it and establish our rhythm of life.* "
> Barbara Hepworth, from *Drawings from a Sculptor's Landscape*, 1966

This makes the achievement of Barbara Hepworth even more astonishing. She was not particularly big or strong. However, like a great sportsperson, Barbara used skill rather than strength. Her carving technique of rhythmic **chiselling** and striking compensated for her slight physique. A journalist in 1950 described her as 'slender, small, dark-haired, and fragile for the **strenuous** work she puts into her 9-hour day'.

Her family was not especially artistic, and her Yorkshire home town was famous for factories rather than sculptures. She had to overcome the **prejudice** of her male teachers and fellow artists against women. And she had to earn a living through her work.

One of Barbara's best-known public works – *Single Form* from 1962 – stands outside the United Nations Building in New York.

Determination and talent

Barbara was driven on by her iron determination to succeed, and by her vast individual talent. She triumphed not only as a woman in a very difficult area of art, but also as a champion of **Modernism**. This revolutionary approach to art, using '**abstract**' forms rather than simply copying from Nature, outraged many people in the first half of the 20th century. But in Barbara Hepworth's sculptures (and drawings) it became a potent and inspiring force, making her an internationally renowned figure. She was undoubtedly one of the most important artists of the 20th century.

The only thing that calms

Barbara Hepworth was dedicated to her work. 'I detest a day of no work, no music, no poetry', she wrote. It was not simply an artist's desire to express herself through sculpture, but a physical and mental need. When she worked, she was completely in charge of her tools and her materials, and freed from the complications of daily life. Work was, to her, 'the only thing that calms'.

This sometimes meant that those nearest and dearest to her felt left out. She could seem cold and neglectful, so wrapped up in her art that she had little time for family or close friends.

Barbara in the lane outside her studio in St Ives. She spent much of her working life in this Cornish town.

One of Barbara's geometric paintings.
She completed many drawings and
paintings besides her sculptures.

But Barbara Hepworth needed to be single-minded. She was a woman in what had always been a man's world of sculpture. To succeed she had to be tough and she had to battle hard to gain recognition, especially when she was beginning her career in the 1920s. Yet she was also expected to take on the role of a traditional wife and mother, responsible for most of the housework and childcare. Although she was able to employ housekeepers and nannies, this must have been a great challenge to her.

No wonder she sometimes found herself torn between the two sides. On the one side, she was a great female artist, certain of her destiny. 'Women are our only hope now,' she said in a BBC interview during the 1960s. They are 'the only people who can help because they are **intrinsically** opposed to destroying life'. Men tried to dominate women, she believed, and turn them into 'hypnotized hens'.

On the other side, Barbara Hepworth was a fiercely dedicated and sensitive woman. 'What a bore it all is being female and alone,' she wrote in her sixties. 'I want to be coddled but I intimidate because I'm efficient and creative. I want to be **maternal** but provoke violent reaction.'

7

A Yorkshire girl

Barbara Hepworth was born on 10 January 1903, in the thriving Yorkshire town of Wakefield. Her parents were determined people – hard-working, careful with money, and eager to better themselves. Her father, Herbert, was an engineer who worked his way up to be the chief **surveyor** of roads and bridges for the County Council. In the office or at home he was a quiet, deeply serious man who rarely smiled or laughed. Barbara totally adored him, and recalled later that 'he only had to look at me with his expressive eyes to quell my misbehaviour'.

Herbert certainly had the strongest influence in shaping his daughter's personality. She was to become fiercely dedicated to work, and anxious to live up to his stern ideals. Barbara's beautiful mother, Gerda, had equally high standards for her children, and pushed Barbara on to excel in her schoolwork. But the strong-willed Barbara often argued with her mother – something she would never have dared to do with her father.

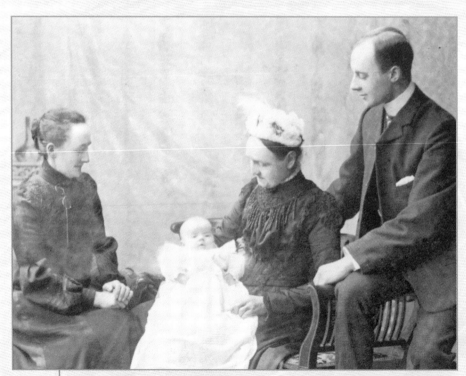

A Hepworth family photograph, taken in 1903. The baby Barbara is held by her great-grandmother, and surrounded by her grandmother and father.

Even at the age of two, Barbara Hepworth seems to stare into the camera with a calm and confident face.

Barbara had two younger sisters, Joan and Elizabeth, and a younger brother, Tony. As the eldest child, she was in a special position, although her father made sure that all of them were treated equally and were given just the same opportunities at school. 'I remember only being loved by my parents,' wrote Barbara. All four children were much loved, also, by the family nanny Kate Ovenden. Strict but cheerful, she made sure that they were well behaved, and gave them each weekend chores (Barbara had to clean out the nursery).

High-school heroine

At the age of five, Barbara Hepworth started at Wakefield Girls' High School. It was to be one of the happiest periods of her life. She wrote later, 'I shall never forget the joy of going to school – and the gorgeous smell of the paint I was allowed to use.' The school gave her not just an education, but the inspiration and encouragement to set out on a career which would make her famous.

Wakefield

Wakefield, with its fine cathedral, had been one of West Yorkshire's chief cities in the Middle Ages. It was famous for the manufacture of woollen cloth, but during the Industrial Revolution of the 18th century, new factories in nearby Leeds and Bradford took over much of this trade.

This was largely due to the headmistress, Gertrude McCroben. 'She knew every one of her 600 girls,' said Barbara, 'and one thing we shared in common was an immense pride in our beautiful school.' Miss McCroben believed passionately that she was preparing her pupils for life, and that girls had to be taught a fighting spirit to enable them to succeed. She also made sure that anyone with a special talent was helped and guided in the right direction.

An exceptional pupil

The young Barbara was a striking figure. With her dignified stride and perfect clothing she seems to have swept rather than walked along the road on her way to school, almost like a princess. Her eyes were dark and piercing, and her forehead high and noble. She stood aloof from the other girls, and had few close friends. Some thought that she put on superior airs, and disliked her.

All the same, she was certainly one of Miss McCroben's favourites. The headmistress quickly saw that Barbara Hepworth was an exceptional pupil, who did well at virtually anything she took up. She won prizes in every subject from Greek and Mathematics to Dancing and Piano. She starred in the school plays, and gained medals in the gym. The one thing she hated was Games, so Miss McCroben allowed her to spend the afternoons in the art room instead.

Barbara at ten years old was already a success in every subject at school – except Games.

A feeling for form

Indeed, art was Barbara's real love. Even as a small child, she had been deeply thrilled by the landscape: 'all my early memories are of forms and shapes and textures'. She recalled car journeys with her father through the Yorkshire countryside where 'the hills were sculptures; the roads defined the form'. She loved 'the sensation of moving physically over the contours, through hollows and over peaks – feeling, touching, seeing, through mind and hand and eye'. It was then that she decided to become a sculptor.

Everyone assumed that Barbara would go on to a glittering career at university. But Barbara herself had different ideas. Still only sixteen, she went to see the

Wakefield Girl's High School, the setting for some of the happiest times of Barbara's life.

headmistress and told her that she did not want to go to university. Instead, she wanted to enter art school and learn sculpture (a very unusual course for a girl at that period). Miss McCroben may have been shocked, but swiftly saw that this was the right choice. 'You can sit for a **scholarship** to Leeds next week!' she said.

Education

At this time, all children in England had to attend school until they were ten years old. The leaving age was only raised to fourteen in 1918 – just as Barbara was leaving school herself. It was not raised to sixteen until as late as 1973. Children were taught a much narrower range of subjects during this period, with little coverage of science or art in many schools. Girls, especially, often learned only about practical things such as cookery and dressmaking, to prepare them for their future roles as housewives.

An expanding world

There had never been an artist in the Hepworth family before. They had been a practical, professional lot, producing engineers, doctors and factory owners. Barbara was different, even as a young schoolgirl. On a trip to London, her mother took her to see the Albert **Memorial**. This huge structure may have been admired by many more conventional people, but Barbara did not care. Taking one look at the famous memorial, she said, 'Oh, how frightful!'

Her **scholarship** to Leeds School of Art for a **foundation course** in 1920 was, therefore, a ticket to a different world. She was later to describe it as 'Leeds and freedom'. There she met people more like herself – people such as Henry Moore, another Yorkshire sculptor destined for greatness, and Edna Ginesi (known as 'Gin'), who became her best friend.

But the course was very hard work. Barbara had to catch an early train from Wakefield every morning, and spend the day learning the skills and theories of the **fine arts**. In the evenings, she went to extra classes in life drawing, not returning home until after 9.30 at night. There was also a sense of rivalry with Moore and her other friends, because each week's drawings would be marked by the lecturer and laid out in order of approval. Barbara, as ever, wanted to be the best.

Going to London

From Leeds, Barbara went out into an even wider world. In 1921 both Barbara Hepworth and Henry Moore gained scholarships to the Royal College of Art in London. It had taken them a single year, instead of the usual two. With Gin and Moore's friend Raymond Coxon they moved to the capital. At first, Barbara lived near the River Thames in a small room, which turned out to be grubby and bug-ridden. She soon found cleaner quarters.

At the Royal College, Barbara was able to concentrate solely on her beloved sculpture for three years. The teaching was still very traditional. Students spent much of their time learning theory or making clay models, from which they could cast their pieces in metal.

But sculpture was changing fast. Young artists were rediscovering the thrill of working directly with stone or wood, using the hammer and **chisel**, responding to the quality of the material while carving. They needed to take great care because each cut removed material permanently; unlike modelling in clay, they could not put a piece back. In this way, they felt that they were being truer to each individual block of material: 'truth to materials' became a rallying cry of the modern sculpture movement.

The coursework was hard. Barbara spent much of the time in her tiny rented studio in the Fulham Road, designing, sketching and modelling. Both she and Henry Moore felt drawn to carving, although it was a very difficult skill to learn, and only a few hours a week were allotted to it. Barbara refused to be put off, and was soon tackling a large stone carving. Although she had to give up this first attempt after a few weeks, her appetite for carving had been awakened.

The eighteen-year-old Barbara Hepworth during her first year at the Royal College of Art in London.

Italian adventure

Student life was not all work. 'Whenever we had saved five pounds we went off to Paris to see museums,' Barbara Hepworth recalled. With her friends she visited the many great galleries and art schools there, sketching and studying pieces by modern sculptors such as Auguste Rodin. Then, in 1924, came the chance for Barbara to enjoy a much longer stay abroad.

A scholarship awarded by the British School in Rome allowed one outstanding art student to live abroad for three years. Barbara decided that she had to win this prize. Battling her way onto the **shortlist**, she entered the final round, working hard to produce a **plaque** made of plaster. But this was not enough for the judges, and she came second. The victor was Jack Skeaping, a student from a rival college.

Although Barbara was bitterly disappointed she still went to Italy, thanks to the award of another scholarship by Yorkshire County Council. The sight of Italy astonished her. 'I arrived in Florence at night,' she wrote, 'with only £9 in my pocket. The light at dawn was so wonderful in the eyes of a Yorkshirewoman who had spent three years in London smog. This new light seized me and I spent one year just wandering and looking everywhere. I wandered round Florence, Siena, Lucca and Arezzo, basking in the new bright light and the new idea of form in the sun.'

Jack Skeaping was a fine musician. Here he plays the accordion, while Barbara accompanies him.

Art in Italy

Italy had been the centre of the great artistic outburst of the Renaissance from the 14th to 17th centuries. Besides being home to talented and skilful architects and painters, it had produced some of the most celebrated of all sculptors, including Donatello and Michelangelo.

Love and marriage

However, Barbara was not travelling alone. In Rome she had met up with her successful rival, Jack Skeaping, and the pair had quickly fallen in love. Brilliant, amusing and bursting with energy, Skeaping was an exciting companion for the reserved Yorkshire girl. He drew, carved, danced, played the banjo, spoke Italian, skated and swam – all with breathtaking natural skill. Barbara and Jack were married in Florence in May 1925.

Over the following months they made a tour of the major towns of Italy, including the capital, Rome. Barbara was deeply impressed as she watched an Italian sculptor showing how marble should be cut, moved and shaped. Soon, she was trying out these techniques for herself, and completing her first successful works in stone.

Doves, from 1927, was one of Barbara's first successful sculptures. It can now be seen at Manchester City Art Gallery.

The first exhibitions

In the summer of 1926 Jack Skeaping fell ill. He and Barbara decided to return home early from Rome and settle in London ('we had to leave behind some wonderful blocks of marble,' she recalled). It was not a good time for little-known artists to earn a living. A **General Strike** had been followed by an **economic down-turn**, and few people had money to spend on the arts. The couple were glad to find somewhere to live and work – a basement flat belonging to a friend in North London.

Barbara and Jack worked desperately hard. While Barbara carried on single-mindedly with her serious sculptures, Jack took on all sorts of jobs besides his carving to make ends meet. He designed pottery animals for Wedgwood, the china manufacturers, and even busked with his accordion, playing for money to people queueing for the theatre. Somehow, they managed to keep going.

A buyer at last

After a year, they held the very first joint exhibition of their work in their flat. It looked like it might bring disappointment – at least, to begin with. Day after day passed, and not a single person came, let alone bought anything. At last, after two weeks, a Rolls Royce pulled up outside the house and out stepped a wealthy Greek collector called George Eumorfopoulos. He purchased three of Barbara's works, including her group *Doves*, and **commissioned** her to carve a seated figure in marble. He also bought some of Jack's sculptures.

Barbara works at a wood carving in the small garden of her North London home, watched by the family dog.

Now that Barbara and Jack were recognized by influential people such as Eumorfopoulos, galleries were more eager to show their work. The following summer, the Beaux Arts Gallery, in London's smart West End, showed sculptures and drawings by Barbara, Jack and a third artist, William Morgan. Many of these were sold, and some drawings ended up in the British Museum. For the first time, the Skeapings had a little money to spare.

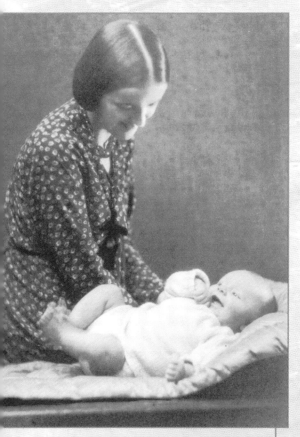

Paul, Barbara's first child, was born in 1929.

Meanwhile, their lives had changed in other ways. In 1928 Barbara and Jack moved to nearby Belsize Park, where they rented one of the purpose-built Mall Studios, with living quarters and a small garden. They soon got to know the other artists working in the neighbouring studios. Then, in August 1929, the Skeapings' first son was born. Barbara remembered this as 'a wonderfully happy time. With [Paul] in his cot, or on a rug at my feet, my carving developed and strengthened.'

New beginnings

'Friends and relations always said to me that it was impossible to be dedicated to any art and enjoy marriage and children,' Barbara wrote much later. She went on to insist that this belief was simply untrue – yet her own life seems to have proved that it was mostly true. Certainly the happy marriage of the Skeapings did not last long after the birth of their son Paul.

Barbara, of course, adored her child. Very quickly, she completed a charming carving called *Infant*, in dark Burmese wood. It showed a baby, upright but in a sleeping position, its little arms held up beside its head. All the same, Barbara did not have the time to look after

Inspired by the birth of her son Paul, Barbara made this wood carving of a sleeping infant.

Paul, so she hired a nurse to tend him while she got on with her work. This irritated Jack, who thought she should have concentrated on the child. The pair began to drift apart, and would finally split up in 1931.

They were really very different kinds of people. Jack worked hard, but he wanted to enjoy himself with social activity – going to parties, dancing, having long conversations, riding horses in the park and motorbikes on the roads. Barbara was totally bound up in her sculpture, and driven on by her need to be recognized as an important modern artist. 'Modern' sculptors were, for the moment, being largely ignored by the press and the large galleries, though Barbara's old friend Henry Moore was becoming a celebrity. Always competitive, Barbara longed to catch up with him.

Fellow Yorkshireman Henry Moore was a lifelong friend – and rival – of Barbara Hepworth.

A breakthrough came in October 1930. Barbara and Jack held a joint exhibition at Arthur Tooth's Gallery in New Bond Street, central London, where they showed nearly 50 pieces in a huge variety of stones and woods. This time the art critics were full of praise for their brilliance and skill in carving. One particularly admired Barbara's little *Infant*.

A different approach

Barbara Hepworth's pieces were clearly different from the work of other young sculptors of the time – who were nearly all men. The sculptures of Henry Moore, for example, were often rugged, tense and weathered. But Barbara's were more soft and sensual, and showed a delight in elegant and harmonious forms.

Meeting Ben Nicholson

Barbara had first met the painter Ben Nicholson at a London gallery. Later, in the summer of 1931, they met again – this time on holiday on the Norfolk coast. Barbara, Ben, Henry Moore (and his new wife), along with other artists and writers had rented a farmhouse at Happisburgh. Here they swam, walked, sketched, played cricket and searched the beach for stones to carve.

Barbara adored the sea, with its ever-changing forms and its timeless strength. When she was a child in Yorkshire, her father had taken the family to stay at Robin Hood's Bay. She remembered that 'the waves thumped on the house and spray fell all around us on the balconies. I was always in a state of great excitement.' Throughout her life, the seaside would always hold a special magic and inspire her in her art.

Now she found another source of inspiration. Ben Nicholson was nine years older than Barbara, a small, bright and very intense character with a lively sense of humour. He had, like her, dedicated his whole life to art. The fact that he was a painter and not a sculptor meant that he was not a rival, as Jack had been, but still someone whose opinion she could respect. 'Each was the other's best critic,' she wrote later.

Barbara and Ben Nicholson on a visit to France

Breaking through

Being in love spurred Barbara on to work even harder, and with greater confidence. Ben moved into the Mall Studios with her (though his first wife refused to divorce him). He in turn was inspired by Barbara's presence: several of his paintings at this time show her or her carvings. In 1932 they held an exhibition together at Tooth's Gallery. A friend, the poet Herbert Read, wrote a foreword to the exhibition catalogue in which he stated that 'among English sculptors, Barbara Hepworth occupies a leading position'.

It was during this period that Barbara made what would later prove to be the most important breakthrough of her career – literally. While

With *Pierced Form* in 1931, Barbara became probably the first British sculptor to 'open up' a piece of work by cutting a hole through it.

working on a small piece of stone, she decided to carve a hole straight through the middle. 'I had felt the most intense pleasure in piercing the stone,' she wrote. The result, later called *Pierced Form*, was a landmark in modern sculpture.

The piercing of the solid form created two important effects. First, it let light into the middle of the sculpture. Secondly, it maintained the outward shape and power of the block from which it was carved. In fact, the continuity between the outside and the inside created an extra tension. This added power and energy could only be seen in an abstract form, and it was a technique that Barbara would continue to employ to great effect in much of her later work.

21

Paris and Picasso

Barbara rarely travelled abroad, but when she did, it affected her deeply. She was normally absorbed by her own work in her own studio, working hard day after day, and having little to do with the outside world. Foreign trips – usually to attend exhibitions – took her out of this routine. They showed her new landscapes, and brought new influences to her art. Her trips to France with Ben Nicholson in 1933 helped her to look at things with fresh eyes.

The couple went first to Paris, where they saw works by some of the most exciting artists of the day, such as the painters Georges Braque, Joan Miró and the sculptor Constantin Brancusi. Later, they visited the most famous of all 20th-century painters, Pablo Picasso, in his studio. 'I shall never forget the afternoon light streaming over roofs and chimney pots through the window onto a miraculous succession of large **canvases**, which Picasso brought out to show us,' Barbara recalled.

Abstract ambitions

Listening to other modern artists and looking at their work inspired Barbara to break away further from tradition. Her experiences on these visits abroad began to push her into more ambitious and adventurous projects. She had reached a crucial point in her sculpting life –

abandoning 'realistic' portrayals of objects, and creating instead purely '**abstract**' forms.

She wrote an article at the time in which she stated her developing ideas. 'I do not want to make a stone horse that is trying to and cannot smell the air. How lovely is the horse's sensitive nose, the dog's moving

Barbara and Ben's home was filled with sculptures and paintings.

Ben plays with the triplets Simon, Rachel and Sarah, who were born in 1934.

ears and deep eyes; but to me these are not stone forms and the love of them and the emotion can only be expressed in more abstract terms. I do not want to make a machine that cannot fulfil its essential purpose, but to make exactly the right relation of masses, a living thing in stone.'

Three more mouths to feed

Barbara was by now pregnant for a second time. One evening in October 1934 she and Ben went to the cinema, then went home with a friend to play cards. Barbara herself seemed tired and withdrawn, but none of them was prepared for what happened next. Barbara's own description sounds strangely like a fairy tale: 'Suddenly I said "Oh dear", and in next to no time I saw three small children at the foot of my bed, looking pretty determined and fairly **belligerent**.'

The unexpected arrival of the **triplets** – Simon, Rachel and Sarah – put a big strain on Barbara and Ben's little household. The couple rented a flat that was separate to their own studios: it was down steps in a basement, with a kitchen that doubled as a bathroom and with no washing allowed in the garden. They had a mere £20 in the bank and no regular income. Barbara's joy at the birth was tempered by the huge demands of three tiny babies. In the end, the triplets were cared for at a nearby nurses' training college, where Barbara could visit them regularly.

The battle for recognition

The birth of the triplets may have been a shock, but it was also a turning-point in Barbara Hepworth's art. Perhaps because of the big change in her life, her work now became almost completely abstract – and increasingly daring – in its use of simple shapes such as spheres, cylinders and hollows. *Discs in Echelon* (1935), for example, consisted of two fat, rounded and highly polished discs of wood standing upright. The stone sculpture *Forms in Hollow* (1935) was made up of three pebble shapes arranged inside a flattened bowl.

Not everybody liked the way Barbara's work was going. More traditional critics sneered at the **modernist** sculptors and painters and their interest in purely abstract works. One dismissed them all as 'a bedful of dreamers', and another went as far as to call Barbara's sculptures 'monstrosities'.

This attitude made life more difficult for Barbara and Ben. Their work was ahead of its time, and buyers were hard to find. For their daily expenses they had to depend on gifts of money from friends and parents (Herbert Hepworth sent something each month).

Hectic home life

It was also a busy time – and getting busier. There were the triplets, who by late 1937 had returned home from the nurses' college and were housed with a nanny next door. There were the regular visitors to entertain, including a solicitor who came down

Barbara in her crowded studio in the Mall, Hampstead, which was now at the centre of an artistic community.

from Yorkshire to buy sculptures, and who had to sleep in a tiny bedroom at the top of a stepladder.

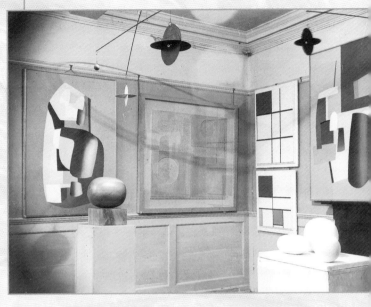

Barbara and Ben were among the artists whose work was shown at the important 'Abstract and Concrete' Exhibition in London in 1936. The sculptures in the foreground of this picture were by Barbara, while Ben's painting is the second from the left.

Then of course there were the neighbours. An increasing number of modernist artists had moved to the Hampstead area. Henry Moore worked just around the corner, and other notable British painters, sculptors and designers were nearby. Europe was in the first throes of the turmoil that was to result in World War II, and several European artists such as Piet Mondrian and Naum Gabo took refuge in North London. Barbara and Ben were at the centre of this growing community, helping to organize exhibitions and run modernist groups.

Ben was divorced in September 1937, and within a few months he and Barbara married at Hampstead Registry Office, not far from the studios. This new sense of security showed in Barbara's work. She was now completing about ten new sculptures each year, and able to concentrate more fiercely than ever. 'Carving became increasingly rhythmical,' she wrote. 'I was aware of the special pleasures that sculptors can have through carving. It seemed to be the most natural occupation in the world.'

All the same, family matters kept pushing their way in. While Ben's studio was always tidy and clean, hers was a jumble of children, rocks, sculptures, wood – and washing. She was delighted to see that the youngsters were prospering and growing up with a great sense of fun. They especially loved the occasions when eccentric neighbours such as Mondrian or Gabo came to tea in their nursery.

Escape to St Ives

By 1938 Barbara was becoming concerned. The clouds of war were gathering, and there was a feeling of uncertainty throughout Britain. Fewer people were risking their money in buying the work of artists – especially **modernists**. Her first answer to the problem was to go even further off the beaten track, to try new directions in her art. She used different materials, stretching strings across the pierced centres of her sculptures, and colouring the interiors with paint. She began to work on much bigger pieces, some of them nearly two metres high. Most of the time she could not afford the materials, but she dreamed of producing huge monuments and made small maquettes (plaster models) of these ideas.

Barbara became increasingly interested in rectangles and straight lines, as can be seen in the *Monumental Stela* of 1936.

In spite of her bold experiments, Barbara needed a bigger change. The studio community at Hampstead (which one writer called 'a gentle nest of artists') was starting to break up. There was a much more serious matter too. By the summer of 1939, World War II was looming, and the threat of bombings made London seem a very dangerous place.

Safety in the south-west

A refuge was offered by Adrian Stokes, a friend and champion of the modernists. He invited the family down to Cornwall for a holiday at his house near St Ives. He added that, if war broke out, the children would be safer there than in a glass-roofed studio in London. But how would they all get there? Barbara and Ben managed to scrape together £17 to buy a battered old car. They tried to persuade Piet Mondrian to come with them, so that they could look after him, but he refused to do so and remained in London, before eventually moving to New York.

Packed with luggage, four adults (including a nanny and a maid) and four children, the car made its long and laborious way across Britain to the far south-west. Barbara was very nervous. Anxious to be in control of her surroundings, she disliked the idea of going to a place she had never seen. Darkness fell, and rain began to lash down as they drove into Cornwall. When they arrived at the Stokes' house it was midnight and, Barbara recalled, 'my spirits were at zero'.

Ideas from abroad

During the 1930s, many Europeans fled to Britain from the harsh governments in their countries – notably Nazi Germany. Some of these asylum-seekers were **avant-garde** artists, who faced persecution at home because the Nazis considered their art to be **degenerate**. Painters like Mondrian and sculptors like Gabo enriched London's artistic world, bringing fresh and challenging ideas about Modernism. Barbara was enthralled by the work of artists such as these, because it seemed to hold out hope of social progress at a time of impending international disaster. She was to carry these ideals with her to St Ives.

Settling in

Next morning Cornwall looked a very different place. Barbara was thrilled by almost everything she could see – the views across the bay, the bright sea, the bare moorland and rugged **tors**, the strange **standing stones** and the abandoned tin mines, and the simple granite cottages of the town itself. Above all, she found St Ives was bathed in its own kind of pure, warm light, which had drawn artists there for more than a century.

Rachel, Simon, Sarah and Paul on the cliffs near St Ives.

At first, all this natural splendour made up for the hectic conditions they were living in. Adrian Stokes and his wife must have been very patient and generous people. Somehow they managed to find room for Ben, Barbara and all their servants and children, plus another couple, in a four-bedroomed house. Meals were a nightmare, with many different needs and dislikes.

But Barbara was cut off from what she loved best – her sculpture. She had no studio, and the only place she could do any work at all was in the Stokes' bedroom. She tried to stick to her old daily routine, though this was not easy. Barbara and Ben were used to sleeping separately, because she liked to smoke in bed. Now they had to share a room. Barbara insisted on setting her alarm clock, which irritated Ben so much that he threw it out of the window.

Making the best of it

'I must do some work,' she wrote despairingly in a letter to a friend. Carving was impossible for the moment, so she turned to drawing. And she could only find time for this in the late evenings and during the night, after the children had gone to bed. Using **gouache** and pencil, she began a series of **abstract** drawings based on simple shapes such as circles, or more complex ones such as crystals. These exercises on flat paper would prove to be a crucial preparation for her sculpture in the years ahead, as she explored the tensions between forms and colours.

By day, there was the problem of making a living, and of raising and feeding the children. Things got slightly easier in early 1940, when Ben and Barbara moved into their own family home nearby. It was very small, but it had a garden, and Barbara set about learning to grow vegetables. Determined and hardworking as ever, she taught herself to dig and sow and hoe – so efficiently that her produce won a prize at the St Ives flower show. She also ran painting and drawing classes for some local children (as well as her own, of course). This was an example of the more gentle and caring side of Barbara's nature – despite her often cold outward appearance, she enjoyed spending time with children and sharing with them her love of art in all its forms.

A studio at last

Money, peace and quiet, room to work, privacy – these things were all crucial to Barbara Hepworth, but they were hard to find in the early months at St Ives. She saw little of Ben in the evenings, for he was often out doing volunteer work as an Air Raid Protection (ARP) warden (there were many German bombing raids throughout the country during this period). Barbara found it a struggle to make ends meet, just selling drawings when she could, to raise cash. The stress and frustration made her sleep badly.

It was not until late 1942 that the family found a bigger home, on a cliff-top near St Ives. Barbara described Chy-an-Kerris as 'a large and very shabby old house'. However, it was big – big enough for Ben and Barbara to have a studio each, and big enough for grown-ups to relax away from the noise of the children. Through her studio window Barbara could watch the ever-changing sea, just as she had watched it when she was a child at Robin Hood's Bay.

'Our work began to flow again,' she wrote delightedly, adding that it was here and now that she produced some of her best pieces. Though not everyone was so pleased. 'I had only limited space: a back yard, a room only eight feet high, and endless complaints about my hammering! The sound of a **mallet** or hammer is music to my ears, when either is used rhythmically, and I can tell by sound alone what is going on. But I could understand how exasperating this could be to neighbours and indeed to the family.'

Housework

The demands of Barbara's family were still heavy. Though Paul was already away at boarding school, the **triplets** were now too old and energetic to be looked after by a nanny. There were serious illnesses. Sarah developed a dangerous disease of the **bone marrow** and, after a long stay in hospital, spent much time in bed or in a wheelchair. And, every day, there were the routine chores of looking after the house. Ben was little help, insisting that his own work came before everything else.

Life was soon to become quieter – perhaps too quiet even for Barbara. Ben announced that he hated winters in Cornwall, and threatened to spend them back in London in future. Meanwhile, Simon, Rachel and Sarah were awarded **scholarships** to attend Dartington Hall, a **progressive** boarding school in Devon. This meant that they were away from home for much of the year.

The war ended at last in 1945. Among the many joys this brought for Barbara was the fact that she could buy stone and other materials more easily. She continued to work, day after day, completing nine major sculptures during 1946, and had a big exhibition in central

London that October. Although works such as *Pelagos* were abstract sculptures, the thrilling St Ives Bay coastline and waves could be recognized as sources of inspiration. The exhibition was a huge success, and one art critic wrote, 'Barbara Hepworth is an extraordinary artist.'

Barbara carved *Pelagos* (meaning 'the sea') from wood, coloured the inside white and attached strings across the topmost curve.

A sort of magic

Towards the end of 1947, Barbara took yet another new path in her art – one which led her back towards the early years. This time she revived her interest in the drawing of human figures. Inviting some young ballet dancers into her studio, she drew very quick sketches as they walked, knelt, sat or exercised. These instant impressions look fresh and vivid, and her concentration on the human form inspired her sculpture too. *Two Figures*, completed in 1948, looks like an **abstract** work, and yet the deceptively simple outlines clearly suggest two people standing side by side.

There was another – and very unlikely – influence on Barbara's new phase. As a result of Sarah's illness, Barbara became interested in the teamwork of medical operations. A brilliant surgeon called Norman Capener invited her to watch him perform operations in hospitals in Exeter and London. Barbara was both scared and excited by the idea, but she put on the gown and gloves and walked into the hospital operating theatre, pen and sketching pad (specially **sterilized**) at the ready.

The peace and clear light of St Ives and the Cornish coast made this the perfect place for Barbara to work.

One of the many drawings which Barbara made of a surgeon at work. She liked to concentrate on the hands.

'I expected that I should dislike it,' she remembered, 'but from the moment I entered I became completely absorbed.' Standing on a box (to give her a better view) and watching the surgeon and nurses at work, she found a strange beauty in the way they moved together, each intent on a single task. It was a subject she was to study and sketch time and time again, attending many more operations and producing over 50 drawings.

A new studio

Of course, sculpture was still at the centre of Barbara Hepworth's art. But the studio at Chy-an-Kerris was not very convenient. It was too small for the big pieces of work, which had to be carved outside in the cold winds. The never-ending sound of Barbara's hammering and chipping annoyed the neighbours, and she herself was frequently distracted by the children. Ben, needless to say, had found himself a studio well away from the house.

So the discovery of Trewyn Studio was, as Barbara put it, 'a sort of magic'. For ten years she had passed the place, as she trudged up and down one of the steep streets of St Ives, little knowing that the perfect setting for her work was hidden behind a high stone wall. It was only when a friend told her that Trewyn was for sale that she went to see it, immediately falling in love with the studio and its pretty garden. She was desperate to buy it and, after a dramatic **auction** (during which Barbara fainted with excitement), Trewyn was hers.

Time to expand

Barbara was so thrilled with her new workplace that she started carving there straight away. So began a fresh routine. Leaving the house each morning, she took a taxi from Chy-an-Kerris to Trewyn. It was an extra expense, to add to the worrying costs of buying and running the studio, but the magic of Trewyn overcame all that. Barbara wrote: 'There I was – space, air, sun and a real proper workshop. The children had their quarters just opposite and Ben his own big studio, and we all began to expand and grow.'

She was now so confident in her work that she even hired an assistant. Denis Mitchell, a cheerful Welsh painter (and one-time tin miner), arrived at the studio in 1949. His job was to help Barbara with the heavy work, **chiselling** the blocks of stone roughly into shape so that she could finish them off exactly as she wanted. Denis was soon at work for five days a week in the studio, where he was eventually joined by other assistants.

Barbara needed these extra hands. She was now nearly 50 years old, and found the sheer physical effort of carving and shifting stone more difficult to cope with. All the same, she felt **diffident** about having to pay helpers, and feared a negative reaction from the press and from rivals. If important visitors arrived at Trewyn, the assistants would sometimes be ushered out of the workshop. Denis and his colleagues also found Barbara difficult to work for at times, because of her unflagging energy and her high-handed attitude.

Artists' assistants

Many artists throughout history have employed assistants to help them with their work. The great Italian Renaissance artist Leonardo da Vinci began his career in the workshop of another painter, where he learned many different skills. Several of Barbara Hepworth's assistants, including Denis Mitchell, went on to become notable artists in their own right.

An artists' colony

St Ives was an ideal base for a sculptor. 'I am so fortunate here to have a garden and space and buildings where I can make such a mess and be tolerated,' Barbara wrote. It was also a town that was quite used to artists and their ways. 'One isn't an oddity, but just another chap rushing out in overalls to buy some more files at the nearest shop.'

By now she had got to know many other artists who had come to live and work in St Ives – especially those interested in **Modernist** ideas, such as Peter Lanyon, Patrick Heron, John Wells and Roger Hilton. Together, Barbara, Ben and the other artists living and working in the area helped to set up the Penwith Society. This society organized exhibitions and other events for the growing artistic community living and working in and around St Ives.

The members of this community shared many concerns with Barbara – for example, how to make art that was both abstract yet which also captured what it meant to experience nature at its most basic. The shared themes – abstraction, landscape, history, the cycles and power of nature – brought the artists and crafts-people of St Ives national and international recognition.

A self-portrait from 1951.

Falling apart

'It is a good thing, perhaps,' wrote Barbara in her short *Pictorial Autobiography*, 'that one does not foresee tragedy ahead. In 1951, after twenty years of family life, everything was to fall apart.' Even years after the event, she found the subject of her split with Ben very painful to discuss. It was her second marriage breakdown, and was to leave her largely alone for the rest of her life.

In fact, they had decided to separate a year earlier. As two sensitive and dedicated artists, working desperately to be recognized and to make a living, they had sometimes found family life too much to cope with. Ben could be difficult and selfish, while Barbara needed a huge amount of encouragement and loving care to be heaped on her, which Ben could no longer provide. Then there was her sculpture, which came before everything else. She had even begun to spend the nights at Trewyn studio, and to stay away from home for days at a time. The two artists were simply no longer compatible.

Now the family had to leave Chy-an-Kerris for good, amid bitter arguments between Barbara and Ben over money. Barbara simply moved her belongings into the studio full-time, while the **triplets** (seventeen years old and about to leave school) were found a little house across the street. Ben remained in St Ives for a few more years, eventually settling in Switzerland in 1958 after marrying for a third time. He died in 1982, seven years after Barbara.

The Festival of Britain

Despite her misery, Barbara somehow slogged on with her work. There were still some moments of magic to lift the gloom – notably a first visit to Venice in 1950. She was invited to exhibit a selection of her recent sculpture at the 25th **Biennale** festival. Venice in midsummer enchanted her, the superb buildings, the ribbons of canal and the flat **lagoon** seeming to make her more aware of the immensity of the sky. She loved watching the endless movement of the people, too, as they walked across the squares and bridges.

Festival of Britain

After the long, grim years of war and rationing, the government decided to hold a 'Festival of Britain' in 1951. This was seen as 'a tonic to the nation' and was centred on a cleared bomb-site on the south bank of the Thames in London. Among the main attractions were the Dome of Discovery (filled with exhibits of the latest styles and technology) and the giant aluminium Skylon, which seemed to stand vertically with no supports. There were also related exhibitions held at venues across the country.

In her St Ives studio, Barbara puts the finishing touches to *Contrapuntal Forms*, which was to feature in the Festival of Britain.

Contemporary art played an important part in the 1951 **Festival of Britain**, and Barbara was among several artists invited to produce work for the site on the south bank of the Thames in London. Her large piece, called ***Contrapuntal*** Forms, was placed proudly next to the most popular place in the Festival, the spiky Skylon tower. Thousands of people from all over Britain visited the site. For the first time in her career, Barbara Hepworth was reaching a mass audience.

International fame

As her celebrity grew, Barbara found herself going forwards – and backwards. The way forwards brought an invitation to help design the **sets** for a production of the Greek play *Electra* at the Old Vic Theatre in London. This was something altogether different, and she was inspired to use new materials – thin steel bars bent into shapes and mounted on a plinth (block or slab). Her set was starkly simple in form – plain columns and flat surfaces – and colour – pure white. 'I loved working on this **commission**,' she recalled.

The way backwards led to Wakefield, her birthplace in Yorkshire. In honour of the **Festival of Britain**, the town mounted an exhibition of her sculpture and drawings at its main art gallery (very near her old school). Barbara now knew very few people in the town, but she was Wakefield's most famous living daughter. There were further exhibitions, too, in London and New York, and a book of her carvings and drawings was published.

Though she was fast becoming a major figure in world art, Barbara's home was now firmly in Cornwall. Despite the upheavals and heartbreak of her separation from Ben, she much preferred to be at Trewyn.

The actress Peggy Ashcroft played the title role in *Electra*, for which Barbara designed the sets.

Here I was in the middle of St Ives with a garden, a yard to work in with sun or moon above, and dreams of large works and freedom of action. Nobody around me has ever complained of the sound of my hammer, I only have to walk 100 yards for the tools I need, and I can wander about in working clothes.

Barbara Hepworth, on the compensations of working alone and undisturbed at Trewyn

She had at last found the perfect place for her work, within easy reach of her great and unfailing sources of inspiration – the sea and the ancient rocks.

Madonna and Child, carved to commemorate the tragic death of her son Paul, was one of Barbara's rare non-abstract works from her later career.

Losing a son

A second and much bigger tragedy struck Barbara early in 1953. Her eldest son Paul (born during her marriage to Jack Skeaping) had qualified as a pilot in the Royal Air Force. That February he was killed in an air crash over Thailand. The news shattered Barbara, but she channelled her grief into her art. The following year she created a carving of the *Madonna and Child* in his memory for the parish church in St Ives.

Looking back

The summer of 1954 saw a major landmark in Barbara Hepworth's career. From April to June, a **retrospective** exhibition of her work, selected from the years since 1927, was assembled at the Whitechapel Gallery in London. Vast stone carvings rumbled their way up from Cornwall, and took their place along with drawings and paintings, all carefully arranged by the sculptor herself.

The exhibition was a huge success. Over 16,000 people visited it, and the closing date had to be postponed for several days to cope with the crowds. Barbara was now so well known that a cartoon of her appeared in the humorous magazine *Punch*. It showed her working away at a sculpture with needle and thread, while underneath was a verse poking fun at her use of stringed and pierced forms:

'I'll never be cultured or decently fed
With holes in my stomach and string in my head.'

Barbara and one of her cats in the garden of Trewyn Studio, with a Hepworth sculpture in the background.

New directions

'This was a most exciting period,' Barbara wrote in her autobiography. Fresh elements gave her the opportunity to experiment and approach her work in different ways. One element was renewed confidence, which came from the triumph of her retrospective at the Whitechapel, and from the success of a travelling exhibition of Hepworth carvings and drawings, which toured North America to great acclaim from 1954 to 1956.

Then there was another brush with the stage – this time opera. The composer Michael Tippett asked Barbara to design scenery and costumes for his groundbreaking new opera, *The Midsummer Marriage*. She stayed in London for the weeks of rehearsals, and dreamed up complex and unusual sets. These included trees made from gauze, barred, net-like shapes, and a mound of blocks and slabs, which one critic likened to 'an intensified timber yard'. The same writer was also full of praise for 'the huge-browed Miss Hepworth, with her firm, precise speech and neat habits of dress'.

The set designed by Barbara for the 'Ritual Dance' section of Tippett's opera *The Midsummer Marriage*.

Finally, there was one of her very rare trips overseas – always guaranteed to refresh and stimulate Barbara. She went on a cruise to Greece. 'The inspiration was fantastic,' she wrote. 'I ran up the hills like a hare, with my notebook, to get there first and have the total impact of solitude.' At the top, she would turn and observe her 199 fellow-cruisers, watching the way they moved. 'Very anti-social, I admit; but I had waited thirty years to get to Greece.'

A gift of guarea

'I looked forward to 1955,' wrote Barbara, 'a year of quiet **abstract** carving.' Indeed, the new year brought ideas and help from all directions. Barbara had barely arrived home from Greece when she learned that a present was waiting for her at Tilbury Docks – and please could she come to collect it! It was a load of seventeen tonnes of guarea (a warm reddish-brown hardwood), all the way from Nigeria – even the smallest piece weighed three-quarters of a tonne.

Somehow, these massive trunks of timber were hauled through the narrow streets of St Ives and into the studio. Barbara got to work with her **chisels** and **gouges** on the beautiful scented wood, which filled the air with its 'savage quality of smell'. She was still burning with inspiration from her trip to Greece, and produced a wonderful series of carvings with Greek titles – *Phira*, *Corinthos*, *Delphi* and *Delos*. 'I was never happier,' she wrote later.

From carving to casting

Even though she had so much splendid stone and wood to carve, Barbara was now looking at new horizons. To make bigger sculptures that would last longer, with more gravity-defying lines, she had to switch to metal – and that meant an entirely different technique. To create a piece in **bronze**, she had to **cast** it. This involved building a clay or plaster model, making a mould (a perfect impression) of this, then pouring molten bronze into the mould.

One of Barbara's finest and most delicate sculptures was *Meridian*, which was cast in Paris. This is a smaller version of the sculpture, called *Garden Sculpture (Model for Meridian)*.

> " *Already one of the largest logs is taking shape – a great cave is appearing within it and I have tunnelled right through the 48 inches and daylight gleams within it. It is terribly exciting to have such enormous breadth and depth. When I have finished perhaps I shall be able to get inside it.* "
> Barbara Hepworth, on how a sculpture was created from the Nigerian 'Great Logs'

Casting brought Barbara a thrilling freedom to experiment. Between 1956 and 1958 she made several soaring, almost airborne, metal pieces. These included *Galliard* (1956) and *Curlew* (1956), for which she bent sheets of brass and strung thick fishing line across the centre. The bronze *Cantate Domino* (1958), at one time exhibited outside the St Ives parish church, stretched heavenwards like a human hand. Other bronzes were inspired by the ebbing and flowing forms of the Atlantic onto the beach, which still bewitched Barbara.

Bartbara always had a strong feeling for the rhythms of the landscape. Here she sits on a rock overlooking moorland near St Ives.

Honours and wealth

After more than 30 years as a sculptor, Barbara at last found herself at the peak of her career. She had money to spend and she had fame, which was fast spreading through much of the world. Her artistic achievement was recognized in the British New Year's Honours List of 1958, in which she became a CBE (Commander of the Order of the British Empire) – just like her father before her. Herbert Hepworth died only a few days later, leaving Barbara desolate.

Another honour arrived in the middle of 1959. Barbara received a telegram all the way from Brazil, announcing that she had been chosen for the Grand Prix (the top prize) at the São Paulo International Exhibition of Modern Art. This was a major award, and gave Barbara huge pleasure – especially as her old friend and rival Henry Moore had won a lesser prize there some years before. And, of course, there was the money: £1600. 'When I got the telegram I wandered about the garden, not believing it!' she said.

The aluminium casting of *Winged Figure* is hauled through the streets of St Ives on its long journey to central London in 1962.

She was now in the middle of a hectic schedule. Quite apart from her beloved work, she had to assemble pieces for the São Paulo show, and for a crucial exhibition in New York.

Barbara always felt very nervous about both exhibitions and travelling by air. Now she felt ill and exhausted. Her doctor knew the signs and would ask her: 'Is this a pre-exhibition or a post-exhibition illness?'

Public figures

All the same, she flew on one of the first jet airliners to the opening of her New York exhibition. It was a triumph. She loved the city, and found that several parties had been arranged in her honour. At one of these she met Dag Hammarskjöld, the popular Secretary-General of the **United Nations**, who bought one of her sculptures. When Hammarskjöld died in a tragic air crash in 1961, Barbara produced one of her finest public sculptures in memory of this great peacemaker. Her *Single Form* (1962) now stands outside the United Nations Building in New York.

Another large piece was for a very public place in England. The firm of John Lewis Ltd **commissioned** Barbara to make a sculpture for mounting on the wall of its new department store in Oxford Street, London. *Winged Figure* (1962) was shaped like a mix between a harp and an angel, and cast strange shadows on the flat bare wall. It was made of aluminium – light enough for its high position in London, but very tricky to handle in the wild Cornish winds while it was being made and transported.

45

Royal patrons

By the early 1960s, Barbara Hepworth had become a national treasure, famous both at home and abroad. Her work had been exhibited throughout Britain and overseas, in galleries, museums and public spaces. There were Hepworth **bronzes** in places as far apart as New York, Jerusalem, Paris and Battersea Park in London. Royalty came to call. The Earl of Snowdon (then married to Princess Margaret) visited Trewyn Studio in St Ives. Queen Elizabeth II bought a Hepworth picture in **gouache**. Queen Ingrid of Denmark attended the opening of a Hepworth exhibition in Copenhagen in 1964.

One result of this fame was that Barbara's prices began to rise dramatically. There was a rapidly growing demand for her sculpture and drawings – so she had to work harder than ever. During the 1960s she finished almost as many pieces as she had in the 1930s, 1940s and 1950s put together – a quite remarkable achievement.

This Hepworth painting of gowned and masked surgeons performing an operation was purchased by Queen Elizabeth II in the 1960s and is now housed in the royal collection at Windsor Castle.

Dance hall to studio

Meanwhile Barbara had also made a much-needed move into bigger premises – just across the road from Trewyn. 'Obtaining a new studio and workshop was a strange experience,' she wrote. 'For many years it had been a Palais de Danse [Dance Hall], with the thump of drums keeping me awake.' Eventually the place went silent. The Palais closed down and the building went on the market.

With a jolt, Barbara suddenly realized that here on her doorstep was a perfect studio and workshop, with a yard for unloading stone and timber, and plenty of storage space. Somehow she found the money (£15,000), rang up the owner and bought it. From a riotous dance hall it was transformed into a haven of peace and quiet. Barbara worked there happily from the moment she took over.

Dame Barbara Hepworth

In 1965 Barbara made her second visit to receive an honour from the Queen at Buckingham Palace, accompanied by her two daughters, now married. This time, she was made a Dame Commander of the Order of the British Empire (DBE). Excited by the whirl of publicity and the pomp of the ceremony, she almost fainted. Her picture appeared in colour supplements, and invitations and congratulations poured in. What pleased her most was being chosen as one of the four artist **trustees** of the world-famous Tate Gallery in London.

The Tate

The Tate in London contains one of Britain's most important art collections. It was founded in the late nineteenth century, and takes its name from Sir Henry Tate, whose family made a fortune from sugar. The collection is now displayed in St Ives and Liverpool as well as at two London sites, the original gallery (now called Tate Britain), and a new gallery at Bankside called Tate Modern.

The final years

Barbara Hepworth was now 62 years old, and her health was beginning to break down. She had smoked cigarettes for much of her adult life, and was found to have cancer and breathing problems. In 1966 she had an operation which kept the disease at bay but left her thin and weak. Unable to eat much, and careless about looking after herself, she became more open to illness and depression.

The next summer she decided to cheer herself up by organizing a holiday with a group of close friends on Tresco, one of the Isles of Scilly. It was meant to be a 'working' holiday, but disaster quickly struck. Barbara already had badly swollen ankles. At the helicopter terminal in Penzance she tripped over and fractured her hip. She took many weeks to recover, and for the rest of her life she had to walk with the aid of walking sticks.

Barbara – with the aid of her sticks – stands at the centre of her retrospective exhibition at the Tate Gallery in 1968.

Becoming a Bard

In the meantime, the honours continued to pile up. There were honorary degrees or doctorates from universities up and down the land – Leeds, Exeter, Birmingham and Oxford. Nearer to Barbara's heart was the ceremony to make her a Bard (outstanding poet or artist) of Cornwall. This took place near St Ives, and she found the ancient rituals 'deeply impressive'. Shortly after this, she was also given the **freedom of St Ives** – another old-established privilege.

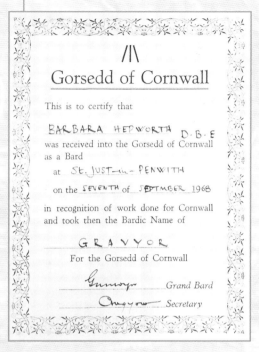

One of Barbara's most prized possessions – the certificate of her reception as a Bard of Cornwall.

/|\
Gorsedd of Cornwall

This is to certify that

BARBARA HEPWORTH D·B·E
was received into the Gorsedd of Cornwall as a Bard

at ST. JUST-in-PENWITH

on the SEVENTH of SEPTEMBER 1968

in recognition of work done for Cornwall and took then the Bardic Name of

GRAVYOR
For the Gorsedd of Cornwall

Grand Bard
Secretary

Perhaps most pleasing of all was the Hepworth **retrospective** exhibition at the Tate Gallery in 1968. This was a major tribute to Barbara's lifetime achievement in the arts, and came exactly 40 years after her very first London exhibition. Never before had so many of her works been brought together in one place. They included over 180 sculptures, loaned from all over the world – Britain, Australia, Brazil, Scandinavia, Germany, Canada and the USA. The event was a huge success, with glowing reviews in the newspapers and enthusiastic crowds packing the gallery.

> " ```
I chose the name 'Gravyor' (sculptor) and it was a memorable moment when this was conferred on me by the Grand Bard of Cornwall. A fitful wind was blowing, but the whole scene was deeply impressive. I shall never forget the sound of singing voices, the cadences of the Cornish language, the sound of pipes, horn and harp. I think the name 'Gravyor' suits me and could well go on my headstone...
> Barbara Hepworth: A Pictorial Autobiography, 1970.

The family of man

Still hobbling, still living alone (her only companions were her cats), Barbara did not expect to live long. She worried about her illness, about her work and about her children. The two girls were happily married and in regular contact with her, but her relationship with Simon was difficult. Mother and son rarely spoke or met. All these anxieties kept Barbara awake at nights, so she was often forced to get up and work or potter about.

However, in 1970 she completed the greatest sculpture of her old age. *The Family of Man* was a massive and ambitious project, especially for someone in poor health. This group of nine bronze figures represented the different ages of a family, from ancestors (3 metres high) to parents and children and then on to what she called the 'ultimate form'. They do not look specifically human, being made up of stark rectangles, crescents and hollows, but they certainly convey human emotions.

Working to the end

Friends and art critics were amazed by Barbara's energy. Pain and frailty made it difficult for her to draw and almost impossible to carve, yet she went on designing, instructing her assistants, and refining her work. In 1972 she began using a new London gallery to display and sell her pieces. At her 70th birthday celebrations a year later, she stayed up late into the night.

The group known as *The Family of Man* – the greatest of Barbara Hepworth's late works.

There were major new sculptures too, in all kinds of material. *Conversations with Magic Stones* (1973), another mysterious group of geometrically shaped bronzes, stood in the garden at Trewyn. *Rock Face* (1973) was a smooth, pierced form in polished stone, while *Small one, two, three* (1975) consisted of three square-faced blocks of marble perched on top of each other.

Death by fire

Throughout all this, Barbara went on smoking heavily. One night in May 1975 she got ready to go to bed at Trewyn, and lit her last cigarette of the day. Then she probably fell asleep. The cigarette dropped from her fingers, setting fire to sheets, papers and then the rest of the house. Neighbours rushed out to see flames and smoke engulfing the old studio. There was nothing they could do to save the elderly woman inside.

Barbara Hepworth had already created a sculpture for her own grave – *Cantate Domino* (1958). But the local council ruled that it was too high (at nearly 2 metres) for the St Ives cemetery, and it ended up in the Tate Gallery. All the same, she was buried in the town she loved so much, and one of her sculptures stands at the entrance to its cemetery.

51

Barbara Hepworth:
the woman and her work

'I think I must have been obsessive and secretive and obstinate from birth, and a difficult child to live with.' Barbara Hepworth wrote this in the introduction to a book of her drawings in 1966, and it is an

Barbara seems dwarfed by her sculptures in the St Ives studio, which became a museum after her death.

> " *In an electric train moving south I see a blue aeroplane between a
> ploughed field and a green field, pylons in lovely **juxtaposition**
> with springy turf and trees of every stature. It is the relationship of
> these things which makes such loveliness.... And I want to project
> my feelings about it into sculpture – not words, not paint, nor
> sound.... It must be stone shape and no other shape.* "
> Barbara Hepworth, 1934

unusually revealing sentence. Generally, she described her life in sunny
and positive terms, brushing unpleasant matters under the carpet.
Yet here she seems to be summing up flaws in her own character
quite honestly.

A single purpose

It is clear that Barbara could be obsessive and obstinate. Her views on
art and life were firm and usually not to be argued with, and she had
little patience with those who did not meet her own high standards.
Fellow artists, workshop assistants, gallery owners and neighbours
(not to mention her family) occasionally found her domineering and
inconsiderate, though she inspired intense loyalty.

She only felt truly alive and fulfilled when she was in her workshop
with **mallet** and **chisel** in hand. Art seemed to release her personality
from the prison of everyday living and allow it to express itself as she
wanted. Sculpture, she said, 'is my whole life, as expressed in stone,
marble, wood and **bronze**'. It was no wonder that work always came
first for her.

An artist's vision

Barbara Hepworth wrote: 'I rarely draw what I see – I draw what I feel
in my body.' This 'feel' – transmitted into her sculptures – was central
to what she created. In fact, it was even more than that: it was central
to her existence. She believed that 'Nothing we touch and feel is
ever lost to us', and retained a crystal clear memory of such things
throughout her life. Sculpture was simply a way of capturing that touch
and feel in physical form.

Barbara Hepworth's influence

Barbara Hepworth drove herself on to succeed brilliantly in sculpture – an area of the arts where men had always ruled. She was not a feminist, but she had very positive views on what was possible for women. 'A woman artist,' she wrote, 'is not deprived by cooking and having children, nor by nursing children with measles (in triplicate) – one is in fact nourished by this rich life, provided one always does some work each day, even a single half hour.'

She thus had an enormous influence on future generations, both because of her gender and because of her genius as an artist. As 'the first great woman sculptor', she was a pioneer in almost unknown territory. Barbara Hepworth's example has been followed by a host of outstanding women sculptors. These include the British artists Elizabeth Frink (who also became a Dame) and Rachel Whiteread, winner of the Turner Prize for Art in 1993.

In recent decades, women sculptors have turned to materials that would have surprised Barbara. The Brazilian Frida Baranek created her sculptures from industrial junk, while Louise Nevelson constructed pieces from wooden objects that were broken or second-hand. The American Magdalena Abakanowicz weaves her sculptures from fibre.

Modernist champion

Of course, Barbara Hepworth was not merely an inspiration to women sculptors. Indeed, her real triumph was as a champion of **Modernism**. She would have rated this as the most important achievement of her career. Modern art was a reflection of modern life

> "
> Barbara Hepworth knew that she was beating a path for women sculptors to follow:
> *I think I can say I was the first in my field to bring the work to a truly professional level. It seems natural now to have several women sculptors round the world, [but] for me it has been a long and uphill fight, and jolly difficult at times.*
> "

(even if, like modern life, it was not always welcomed) in which political and social ideals could be pursued. It was this moral aspect of Modernism which most appealed to her.

Along with Ben Nicholson and others, Barbara Hepworth spearheaded the development of **abstract** art in Britain, and introduced the startling idea of the 'hole' in sculpture with her *Pierced Form* of 1931. In doing so, she added to the growing international understanding of the new art and its new language. 'We may have lived at St Ives,' she wrote, 'but we were in close contact with the whole world.'

The Sculpture Gardens within the Barbara Hepworth Museum in St Ives. The museum is located in Barbara's Trewyn Studio and is run by the Tate.

Timeline

1903	Barbara Hepworth born on 10 January in Wakefield, Yorkshire, England.
1908	Begins school at Wakefield Girls High School.
1910–12	The post-Impressionist era is introduced to London, paving the way for **Modernism**.
1914–18	World War I.
1920	Barbara wins **scholarship** to Leeds School of Art for **foundation course**. Meets Henry Moore.
1921	With Moore, wins scholarship to Royal College of Art in London.
1923	Barbara and friends visit art galleries and museums in Paris.
1924	Barbara produces a relief for the Prix de Rome competition. Gains travelling scholarship from Yorkshire County Council to study in Italy. Meets Jack Skeaping.
1925	Barbara and Jack marry in Florence. **General Strike** in England. Jack falls ill and the pair return to London
1927	First exhibition, held in Barbara and Jack's studio in St John's Wood.
1928	With William Morgan, Jack and Barbara exhibit works at the Beaux Arts Gallery in Bond Street, London. Barbara and Jack move to studios in Belsize Park, London.
1929	Son Paul is born.
1930	Barbara shows sixteen pieces of sculpture at Tooth's Gallery, London.
1931	Split between Jack and Barbara. Barbara meets Ben Nicholson at Happisburgh, Norfolk. Barbara begins experimenting with 'pierced' forms (forms with holes).
1932	Barbara and Ben hold joint exhibition at Tooth's Gallery.
1933	Nazis take power in Germany, alarming Europe. Visit to Paris with Ben; they meet several modernist artists, notably Picasso. Barbara abandons sculptures of figures for a decade.

1934 **Triplets** Simon, Rachel and Sarah are born. They are cared for at a nurses' training college near Barbara and Ben's home.

1935 Barbara takes part in an **abstract** art exhibition in Oxford, Liverpool, London and Cambridge.

1936 International Surrealist Exhibition shocks London.

1937 Barbara contributes essay on sculpture to the influential Modernist book *Circle*. Triplets return, and live with nanny.

1938 Ben and Barbara marry.

1939 Barbara begins using colours and stringed centres in her work. Outbreak of World War II. Danger of bombing causes Barbara and family to move to St Ives, Cornwall, to stay with friends.

1940 The family move to a small house of their own. Barbara learns how to grow vegetables and runs art classes for children.

1942 A bigger house is found: Chy-an-Kerris.
Barbara produces a series of geometrical drawings.

1943 Sarah has long stay in hospital with **bone marrow** infection.

1945 World War II ends.
Barbara produces works inspired by the Cornish coastline.

1947 Barbara's interest in drawing, especially of figures, is renewed. She attends and sketches scenes in operating theatres.

1949 Buys Trewyn Studio in St Ives and hires Denis Mitchell, her first assistant.
Continues series of figure drawings.

1950 Barbara and Ben decide to separate. Barbara shows sculptures and drawings at the Venice **Biennale**, which she visits.

1951 Barbara leaves Chy-an-Kerris to live in Trewyn.
Barbara is **commissioned** to do two large sculptures for the **Festival of Britain** in London. Marriage to Ben Nicholson is dissolved.
Exhibition at Wakefield City Art Gallery.
Designs **sets** and costumes for Old Vic production of *Electra*.

1953 Gains a second prize in an international sculpture competition on the theme of 'The Unknown Political Prisoner'.
Son Paul Skeaping is killed in an air crash.

1954 **Retrospective** exhibition at Whitechapel Art Gallery, London. Barbara takes holiday cruise to Greece.

1955 A present of guarea wood inspires a series of carvings. Barbara designs set and costumes for Tippett's opera *The Midsummer Marriage*.
Hepworth exhibition tours museums in USA and Canada.

1956 Turns to **casting** pieces in **bronze** and other metals. Produces *Curlew*, a metal sheet and fishing-line stringed figure.

1958 Created Commander of the Order of the British Empire (CBE).

1959 Gains major prize for sculpture at São Paulo Biennale, Brazil.

1960 Awarded honorary degree at Birmingham University.

1961 Awarded honorary degree at Leeds University.
Commissioned to produce *Single Form* as a **memorial** to Dag Hammarskjöld.

1962 *Winged Figure* is commissioned by John Lewis Ltd for Oxford Street store.

1963 Given 'The Foreign Minister's Award' at the Tokyo Biennale.

1964 Hepworth exhibition tours Scandinavia.
Buys the Palais (dance hall) opposite Trewyn as a workshop.

1965 Created Dame Commander of the Order of the British Empire (DBE).

1966 Awarded honorary degree at Exeter University.
Undergoes operation for cancer.

1967 Falls and fractures hip.

1968 Awarded honorary degree at Oxford University.
Made a Bard of Cornwall, and given the **freedom of St Ives**.

Major retrospective exhibition at the Tate Gallery in London.

1970 Creates *Family of Man* group of bronzes.

1973 70th birthday celebrations in St Ives.

1975 Dies in an accidental fire at Trewyn Studio.

1976 Barbara Hepworth Museum and Sculpture Garden, a private museum funded by the family, opens in St Ives.

1980 Hepworth **trustees** and family give the Museum and art collection to the nation. It becomes part of the Tate Gallery.

Glossary

abstract style of art that does not depict scenes or objects realistically, but deals in pure forms and colours

auction public sale at which property is sold to the person who places the highest bid (offers the most money)

avant-garde experimental and new

belligerent quarrelsome or aggressive

Biennale festival or other event which takes place every two years (from the Italian word meaning 'bi-yearly')

bone marrow tissue contained inside bones that helps in the formation of blood cells

bronze alloy (mixture) of mainly copper and some tin – 'a bronze' refers to a sculpture made of bronze

canvas material usually used as a support for oil paintings – the word can also mean the painting itself

cast (verb) to make a plastercast model using a mould; (noun) a sculpture made from a cast

chisel (noun) metal tool with a flat sharp edge for shaping materials; (verb) the action of using a chisel

commission (verb) to place an order for something to be made; (noun) an article that has been commissioned

conscious awake and aware of one's own existence and feelings

contour line on a map that shows height

contrapuntal combining two or more lines in a form to create contrasts in balance or shape

degenerate corrupt and immoral

detest violently dislike or hate

diffident modest or shy

economic down-turn major fall in the economy of a country, with an accompanying decline in business and employment

Festival of Britain nationwide celebration organized in 1951 to demonstrate how Britain had developed since World War II

fine arts the 'visual' arts – painting, drawing and sculpture – as opposed to the other arts – literature, music, etc.

foundation course one-year course that prepares art students for a degree course

freedom of the city special privilege or honour given to a public figure in recognition of their achievements

General Strike widespread strike by workers in many British industries in 1926

gouache type of water colour, sometimes mixed with gum

gouge type of chisel, with a rounded blade

inanimate showing no signs of life or movement

intrinsically essentially, or completely

juxtaposition placing of two things side by side, or close to each other, often to show the contrast between them

lagoon body of salt water separated from the sea

mallet hammer with a wooden head, used with a chisel

maternal motherly, or like a mother

memorial object or composition created in memory of someone who has died

Modernism wide range of experimental trends in the arts that began in the early 20th century

plaque flat plate, often engraved or decorated for mounting on a wall

prejudice unreasonable dislike or suspicion of a group, gender or race

progressive moving forward, and believing in continual improvement or change

retrospective an exhibition that looks back, showing products from the whole range of an artist's career

scholarship award of financial aid to help a student in education

set scenery and setting designed for an opera or play

shortlist reduced list of possible candidates for a position or prize, from which a final winner is chosen

standing stones large stones set up on end, singly or in groups, during neolithic times (the Stone Age)

sterilized treated, either with heat or chemicals, to kill all bacteria and other organisms

strenuous requiring great effort or strength

surveyor a person trained to value land or buildings

thrifty careful with money; frugal and hard-working

tor rock or pile of bare rocks on top of a hill

triplets three babies born at the same time

trustee person who is elected or appointed to control the funds or policy of an institution

United Nations international organization of independent countries, formed in 1945 to help bring about worldwide cooperation and peace

Further reading, places of interest and websites

Further reading

Most of the following books are written for adults, but may also contain material of interest to student readers, too.

Barbara Hepworth, A. M. Hammacher (Thames and Hudson, 1968)
Barbara Hepworth, Penelope Curtis (Tate Gallery Publishing, 1998)
Barbara Hepworth: Early Life (Wakefield Art Gallery, 1985)
Barbara Hepworth: A Life of Forms, Sally Festing (Viking, 1995)
Barbara Hepworth: A Memoir, Margaret Gardiner
   (Salamander Press, 1982)
Barbara Hepworth: A Pictorial Autobiography (Adams and Dart, 1970)
Barbara Hepworth: A Retrospective (Tate Gallery Publishing, 1994)
*Barbara Hepworth: Works in the Tate Gallery Collection and the
Barbara Hepworth Museum St Ives*, Matthew Gale and Chris Stephens
   (Tate Gallery Publishing, 1999)
British Sculpture in the Twentieth Century, edited by Sandy Nairne and
   Nicholas Serota (Whitechapel Gallery, 1981)
Dictionary of British Art, edited by David Bindman (Thames and
   Hudson, 1985)
Drawings from a Sculptor's Landscape, Barbara Hepworth
   (Cory Adams and Mackay, 1966)

Places of interest

*Barbara Hepworth Museum and Sculpture Garden, Barnoon Hill,
St Ives, Cornwall* – the artist's studio contains a huge number of her sculptures and drawings. It is now run as part of the Tate, through Tate St Ives. Opening times vary according to the season.

Tate (Tate Britain, Tate Modern) – both of these London museums show notable Hepworth pieces from the Tate collection.

Aberdeen Art Gallery, Birmingham Art Gallery, Bristol City Art Gallery, Leeds City Art Gallery, Manchester City Art Gallery, The Scottish National Gallery of Modern Art (Edinburgh) and Wakefield City Art Gallery – all of these galleries have Barbara Hepworth collections that are worth visiting.

There are also works by Barbara Hepworth on display in many cities worldwide, including Melbourne, Sydney (Australia); São Paulo (Brazil); Ottawa, Toronto (Canada); Detroit, Minneapolis, New York, St Louis, Syracuse, Washington D.C. (USA); Copenhagen (Denmark); Helsinki (Finland); Otterlo (Netherlands).

Websites

There is no website specifically devoted to Barbara Hepworth, though one is planned. However, there are thousands of entries about her and her work on the internet. Useful ones include:

www.artcyclopedia.com

www.artnet.com

www.tate.org.uk

Index

Titles in the *Creative Lives* series include:

Hardback   0 431 13997 0

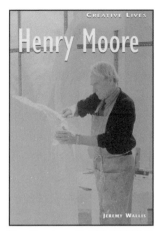

Hardback   0 431 13984 9

Hardback   0 431 13994 6

Hardback   0 431 13996 2

Hardback   0 431 13998 9

Hardback   0 431 13995 4

Hardback   0 431 13999 7

Find out about the other titles in this series on our website www.heinemann.co.uk/library